W9-ABY-402

Big Bang SCIENCE EXPERIMENTS

MATERIAL WORLD

THE SCIENCE OF MATTER

Jay Hawkins

WINDMILL BOOKS™

New York

Published in 2013 by Windmill Books, An Imprint of Rosen Publishing
29 East 21st Street, New York, NY 10010

First Edition

Editors: Joe Harris and Samantha Noonan
Illustrations: Andrew Painter
Step-by-Step Photography: Sally Henry and Trevor Cook
Science Consultant: Sean Connolly
Layout Design: Orwell Design

Picture Credits:
Cover: Getty Images (Edward Kinsman/Oxford Scientific)
Interiors: Javier Trueba/MSF/Science Photo Library: 4–5. Shutterstock: 22 (Potapov
Alexander), 26 tr (Rashevska Natalia).

Library of Congress Cataloging-in-Publication Data

Hawkins, Jay.
 Material world : the science of matter / by Jay Hawkins. — 1st ed.
    p. cm. — (Big bang science experiments)
 Includes index.
 ISBN 978-1-4777-0323-6 (library binding) — ISBN 978-1-4777-0367-0 (pbk.) — ISBN
978-1-61533-671-5 (6-pack)
 1. Materials—Experiments—Juvenile literature. 2. Science—Experiments—Juvenile
literature. I. Title.
 TA403.2.H39 2013
 530.078—dc23
                                        2012026221

Printed in China

CPSIA Compliance Information: Batch #AW3102WM: For Further Information contact Windmill Books, New York, New York at 1-866-478-0556
SL002561US

CONTENTS

This book must really "matter!"

CAVE OF WONDERS

The Crystal Cave, in northern Mexico, is home to some truly amazing natural formations. The biggest crystals found there are 50 feet (15 m) long! This book is full of facts and experiments exploring the incredible science of materials.

CRYSTAL COLUMNS

These enormous crystal pillars formed hundreds of thousands of years ago, as water containing a mineral called gypsum filtered through the caves.

MAGMA MAGIC

At first the water was heated by underground magma. As the magma cooled, the minerals formed selenite molecules, which joined together into enormous crystals.

PERFECT PATTERNS

The properties of materials are dictated by their molecular makeup. Like all crystals, these enormous pillars have a shape that echoes the shape of the molecules that make them up at a microscopic level. The molecules inside are organized in neat, repeating patterns.

GLOOPY GOOP

This strange slime is not really a liquid, but not really a solid either! Make some for yourself to find out what sort of material it is.

Step 1

Pour a cup of cornstarch into a mixing bowl. How does the cornstarch feel?

Step 2

Add two drops of food coloring to the water. You really don't need very much!

Step 3

Mix the water into the flour, using your fingers. How does the mixture feel?

Step 4

Try squeezing a handful of liquid you've made into a ball. It will become a solid!

Step 5

Let the goop settle into the bottom of the bowl. Touch the surface gently, then tap it hard.

Step 6

If you hold your hand still, it will become liquid and run through your fingers.

My goop has come to life! I think I'll call him "Bob."

How do you do?

HOW DOES IT WORK?

When this mixture is put under pressure, the cornstarch molecules are forced together, and it behaves like a solid. When it is handled gently, the cornstarch molecules can move around freely, and it flows like a liquid.

MAKE YOUR OWN LAVA LAMP

Lava lamps are always fascinating to watch. Now you can make your own!

YOU WILL NEED

- ★ A clean plastic bottle or jar
- ★ Funnel
- ★ Vegetable oil
- ★ Food coloring
- ★ Effervescent vitamin tablet
- ★ Flashlight
- ★ Water

Step 1

Fill a bottle or jar ¼ full with water. Add 10 drops of food coloring.

Step 2

Fill the bottle to the top with vegetable oil.

Step 3

Break the vitamin tablet into four pieces.

Step 4

Drop one piece of the vitamin tablet into the bottle and watch the result.

Step 5

To improve the lava lamp effect, turn off the lights, switch on the flashlight, and shine it through the bottle.

I really "lava" this experiment!

Experiment with different jars and bottles and other food colorings. Which work the best?

You can restart your lava lamp by adding another tablet.

HOW DOES IT WORK?

Oil and water do not mix. When you add oil to water it usually just sits on its own in a separate layer on top of the water. However, adding the bit of tablet to the container changes this. The tablet reacts with the water, creating bubbles of carbon dioxide gas which rise to the surface. The oil and water are stirred up by the bubbles.

CANDY VOLCANO

Get ready for an edible eruption! In this experiment, you'll discover that mixing soft-centered mints and diet cola can have explosive results.

WARNING!

Ask an adult to help you with the hot water.

YOU WILL NEED

* ★ Two packets of strawberry flavored gelatin
* ★ A packet of soft-centered mints
* ★ Hot water
* ★ A large mixing bowl
* ★ A small glass
* ★ A can of diet cola
* ★ Plate
* ★ Tray

Step 1

Take two packets of gelatin. Follow the instructions on the packets to make a gelatin mixture.

Step 2

Take a big bowl. Turn a glass upside down inside it.

Step 3

Pour the gelatin mixture into the bowl. Make sure it covers the glass.

Step 4

Put the gelatin in the fridge to set. When the gelatin has set, turn it out onto a flat plate and remove the glass.

Step 5

Put the plate onto a tray. Take the gelatin outside and pour diet cola into the cavity left by the glass.

Drop six soft-centered mints into the cola. Watch out—it will erupt!

KABOOM!

Add more cola if you want.

This experiment is good enough to eat... if you're brave enough!

HOW DOES IT WORK?

The bubbles in a cola drink are made up of carbon dioxide gas. They have been forced into the drink under pressure. When you drop a soft-centered mint into the soda, the carbon dioxide bubbles collect together and grow in the tiny dents on the surface of the mint. Then the bubbles rush out in an eruption.

MAKE A BALLOON KEBAB

You can't stick a sharp object through a balloon without popping it. Right? Wrong! Amaze your family and friends by making a genuine balloon kebab.

Step 1

Blow up a balloon to about half its full size, and tie a knot in the neck.

No one will believe these results—but it really works!

Step 2

Hold the balloon in one hand and the kebab skewer in the other.

14

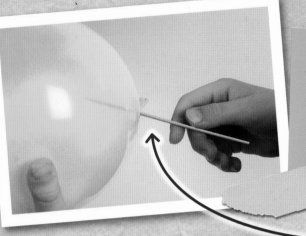

Step 3

Poke the point of the skewer into the the balloon, near the knot.

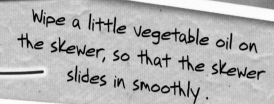

Wipe a little vegetable oil on the skewer, so that the skewer slides in smoothly.

Step 4

Push the skewer through the balloon very gently, twisting as you push. Aim to make it come on the opposite side, at the middle of the top of the balloon.

Step 5

If you have a long skewer, or small balloons, try to add more balloons—like a kebab!

Step 6

If you poke the balloon in the middle with the skewer, it will pop.

HOW DOES IT WORK?

Normally, when a balloon is stabbed with a kebab skewer, the rubber skin will tear and it will pop. That is because the pressurized air inside the balloon is stretching the skin very tight, so that the slightest hole blows open in an instant. However, the skin is not as tight at the "ends" of a balloon. So stabbing it there won't pop it—as long as you're careful.

MAGNETIC CEREAL

Is the iron contained in food the same thing as the metal iron? Try this experiment to find out.

YOU WILL NEED:

★ Cereal fortified with iron (look at the small print on the box)

★ A rolling pin

★ A small plastic bag

★ A very strong magnet—a "rare earth" magnet will work well

★ A cereal bowl

★ Water

Step 1

Crush some cereal into a fine powder in a small bag.

The bag keeps the cereal together.

Oh no! Keep that magnet away from me!

Step 2

Put the magnet in the powder and roll it around.

Step 3

Take the magnet out of the bag. It should have crumbs of cereal sticking to it.

Try shaking the powder off-the magnetic attraction won't let you!

Step 4

Take a clean cereal bowl and fill it almost to the top with water.

Step 5

When the water has stopped any movement, drop a large flake of cereal on the surface, in the middle of the bowl.

Step 6

By holding your magnet just above the cereal flake, you should be able to draw it across the surface of the water without touching it!

HOW DOES IT WORK?

This experiment shows that fortified cereals, like many other foods, contain iron in small amounts. It is very important that you get enough iron in your diet. Iron helps your blood to carry oxygen around the body. If you don't have enough of it, you may feel tired and unwell.

BUBBLE BOMB!

YOU WILL NEED:

★ Water

★ A measuring cup

★ A sealable plastic bag

★ Paper towel

★ 2 tablespoons of sodium bicarbonate

★ Vinegar

This fun and safe "bomb" will explode with a loud pop!

Step 1

Find a place where making a mess won't be a disaster—outside, or perhaps the bathroom if the weather's bad.

Step 2

Test your bag for leaks. Put some water in it, close the seal and turn it over. If no water leaks out, it's okay to use.

Step 3

Tear a small piece of paper towel, about 5 inches (13 cm) square. Put 2 tablespoons of sodium bicarbonate in the center of the square and fold the paper towel around it.

Get ready for a bubble BOOM!

Step 4

Mix 10 fl oz (300 ml) of vinegar and 5 fl oz (150 ml) of warm water and pour them into the plastic bag.

Step 5

Put the paper towel packet into the bag and hold it in the corner away from the vinegar while you seal the bag.

Step 6

Place the bag on the floor and stand well back!

Step 7

The bag will swell up...

Step 8

...and then pop!

HOW DOES IT WORK?

Vinegar is an acid and sodium bicarbonate is a base. When you mix acids and bases together, they react and turn into different chemicals. They usually turn into a salt and water, and in some cases, they also form a gas. When carbon dioxide gas forms in our experiment, there is not enough room for it in the plastic bag. So the pressure builds up and the bag swells until it pops and releases the gas.

CRYSTAL SHAPES

You don't have to go down a mine to find colorful crystals. In fact, you can grow them at home!

YOU WILL NEED

★ Salt and water
★ Cotton thread and scissors
★ Saucepan
★ A spoon
★ Clean, empty jars
★ Pipe cleaners
★ Pencils

Step 1

Twist a pipe cleaner into a shape, such as a star or circle. Tie some cotton threads across the shape to make a web. Tie a thread about 2 inches (5 cm) long to the top.

Step 2

Fill your jar ¾ full of water. Pour the water into a saucepan. Ask an adult to heat the water on the stove until it's starting to boil.

Step 3

Turn the heat down and start adding salt to the water. Stir in the salt until you can't get any more to dissolve.

WARNING!
You will need adult supervision when boiling water.

Step 4

Ask an adult to pour the solution into a jar.

Step 5

Tie the thread on your pipe cleaner shape to the middle of a pencil. Then lower the shape into the jar, so that the pencil rests on the sides of the jar.

It's crystal clear to me that these crystals are clear!

Step 6

Repeat the process with different shaped pipe cleaners. Then leave them for two days. Can you see crystals beginning to form?

Step 7

Your crystals will continue to grow for a week. When you have finished growing them, you can hang your shapes up as decorations!

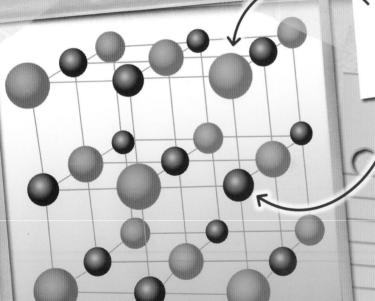

= Chlorine

= Sodium

The molecules in a salt crystal are made up of two elements: sodium and chlorine. Both elements are poisonous on their own, but when combined together, they make a tasty seasoning for food!

HOW DOES IT WORK?

More salt can dissolve in hot water than cold water. As the salty water cools, some of the salt is forced to leave the solution. Those salt molecules join together into crystals. Salt crystals have a cube shape, which reflects the shape of salt molecules, which are also cubes (see the picture on the left).

RAINBOW CABBAGE

As we saw in the "Bubble Bomb" experiment (pages 18-19), reactions between acids and bases can be really explosive! But how can you tell if something is an acid or a base?

YOU WILL NEED:

★ Red cabbage
★ A cheese grater
★ Boiling water
★ A sieve
★ 2 pitchers
★ 5 glasses
★ Blotting paper
★ Vinegar, sodium bicarbonate, a lemon, and dishwashing liquid

Step 1

Ask an adult to help you grate a cupful of red cabbage.

Step 2

Put the grated cabbage in a pitcher. Ask an adult to pour in about a pint of boiling water.

Step 3

When the water has cooled, pour it through a sieve. You will be left with a purple liquid. This is your indicator.

Step 4

Collect together a lemon, some vinegar, some sodium bicarbonate, and some dishwashing liquid.

The color of the indicator depends on the acidity of the water.

Step 5

Pour equal amounts of liquid in each glass.

Make a note of each substance.

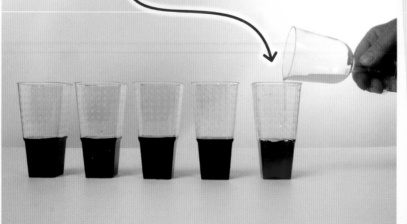

Step 6

Pour vinegar into one of the glasses, until you see a color change. Then squeeze lemon juice into another glass. Add sodium bicarbonate and dishwashing liquid to another two glasses.

Step 7

Put a strip of blotting paper in each glass to soak up the liquid.

Step 8

You should see a rainbow of different colors. Acids will turn the cabbage juice indicator red. Bases will turn the cabbage juice blue, green, or even yellow.

Bicarbonate of soda | Indicator | Washing up liquid | Vinegar | Lemon juice

I wonder if this little guy is an acid or a base!

HOW DOES IT WORK?

Red cabbage contains a molecule called "flavin." This is what reacts with the different substances. Acids turn our flavin-rich solution red, and bases turn it blue, green, or yellow.

COIN CLEANER

YOU WILL NEED

* ★ Dirty coins
* ★ Cola
* ★ A plastic cup
* ★ A paper towel
* ★ Old toothbrush

Many people like to collect coins from different countries. However, coins tarnish easily, and can soon start to look dirty. Here is how you can give them back their shine.

Step 1

Take some dirty coins. Why not take a photograph to compare results later on?

Step 2

Rinse a coin in water to remove loose dirt.

Step 3

Put the coin in a plastic cup and pour in some cola.

Step 4

After 20 minutes, take the coin out and dry it.

Step 5

Repeat the process until the coin is clean. With a really dirty coin, it may help to agitate the cola on the coin with an old toothbrush.

Step 6

Take pictures of your coin at intervals to see the rate of change. Here's a very dirty old coin, showing results after 30 mins, 2 hours, 6 hours, 12 hours, and a day.

These clean, shiny coins really look like a million dollars!

HOW DOES IT WORK?

Cola drinks are more acidic than you might think! The cola is corroding away the top layer of the coins. That makes them look clean.

MAGICAL MYSTERY BOX

YOU WILL NEED

- ★ A cardboard box with a lid
- ★ Two pieces of cardboard as long and wide as the box
- ★ Some materials with different textures
- ★ Scissors and tape
- ★ A dark-colored plastic bag
- ★ Saucers
- ★ Paint and markers
- ★ Friends to help

Can you and your friends identify materials by touch alone? This fun experiment shows just how much we normally rely on sight, hearing, smell, and taste to identify materials.

Step 1

You will need a cardboard box that opens at the top.

Step 2

Use two pieces of cardboard to divide the inside of your box into four parts.

Step 3

Cut a hole on each side of the box, just big enough to get a hand into each compartment.

Step 4

Use scissors to cut squares about 4 inches (10 cm) long from a plastic bag. Tape the top edges above each hole inside the box.

Step 5

Put four different materials onto saucers and place a saucer in each compartment of the box.

marbles

baked beans

mints

grapes

Step 6

Now your friends can take turns to feel in the box and guess what the material is. Write down their guesses.

Your friends might think some materials feel weird or gross.

You can decorate your box if you like.

HOW DOES IT WORK?

We normally identify materials by studying many different properties. In this experiment, you are only able to study their texture and temperature. That makes it harder!

GLOSSARY

acid (A-sud) A chemical substance with a sour taste and, if strong enough, able to eat away at other substances.

base (BAYS) A chemical substance that can reverse the effects of an acid; like an acid, it can eat away at other substances if it is strong enough.

crystal (KRIS-tul) An object formed from solid forms of chemical elements, often nearly clear and with even, flat surfaces.

effervescent (eh-fer-VES-sent) Fizzing or creating bubbles.

element (EH-luh-ment) A substance, such as iron or oxygen, that cannot be broken down into other substances using ordinary chemical processes.

eruption (ih-RUP-shun) An explosion caused when something bursts out of a contained area very quickly.

fortified (FOR-tih-fyd) Strengthened, often by adding other substances to improve our health.

magma (MAG-muh) Liquid rock beneath the Earth's surface.

mineral (MIN-rul) A substance, such as most rocks, that has never been a living material.

molecule (MAH-lih-kyool) A group of atoms bonded together to form what is known as a chemical compound. A molecule is the smallest particle that still has all of the chemical properties of a substance.

pressurized (PREH-shuh-ryzd) Receiving a constant high force .

selenite (SEH-lih-nyt) A mineral that forms large crystals.

solution (suh-LOO-shun) A mixture of two substances, one of which is dissolved in the other.

tarnish (TAR-nish) To change color and become duller-looking, usually after exposure to air or other substances.

Oh, so THAT's what that word means!

30

FURTHER READING

Brasch, Nicolas. *Tricks of Sound and Light.* The Science Behind. Mankato, MN: Smart Apple Media, 2011.

Graham, Ian. *Science Rocks!* New York: DK Publishing, 2011.

Green, Dan. *The Elements: The Building Blocks of the Universe.* Discover More. New York: Scholastic Reference, 2012.

Hill, Lisa. *The Properties of Elements and Compounds*. Chicago: Heinemann-Raintree, 2009.

Hirsch, Rebecca. *Properties of Matter*. Ann Arbor, MI: Cherry Lake Publishing, 2012.

Knight, Erin. *Chemistry Around the House*. New York: Crabtree Publishing, 2011.

O'Neal, Claire. *A Project Guide to Matter*. Hockessin, DE: Mitchell Lane, 2011.

TIME for Kids. *TIME for Kids Super Science Book*. New York: TIME for Kids Book, 2009.

Wheeler-Toppen, Jodi. *Cool Chemistry Activities for Girls*. Mankato, MN: Capstone Press, 2012.

Websites

For web resources related to the subject of this book, go to: www.windmillbooks.com/weblinks and select this book's title.

INDEX

I think this is soda-or is it lava?

Whatever it is, don't drink it!